Castles

Written by Maggie Freeman

Illustrated by Pat Murray and Mike Phillips

Contents

Collins

Why did people build castles?

Rich people built castles so they would have somewhere safe to live.

People piled up earth and stones where there were no hills or sea. They dug moats and filled them with water.

▲ Clifford's Tower, York

▼ Bodiam Castle, East Sussex

5

Keeping safe

You could see a long way from the top of a castle …
but it was windy and cold up there.

It was safe inside the castle and people liked to shelter there from danger. It got very crowded if the animals went in too. Some castles only had space for soldiers.

The outside walls were often four metres thick.

The towers stuck out so soldiers could see to shoot at the enemy at the bottom of the wall.
At the top of the walls and towers were battlements. These had crenels which soldiers could shoot through in battles.

▲ *Bodiam Castle, East Sussex.*

Swinging wooden shutters in the crenels were useful in battle.

tower

battlements

crenel

thick walls

crenel

wooden shutter

9

Attack!

There were lots of ways of attacking a castle,
but it was very difficult to break in.

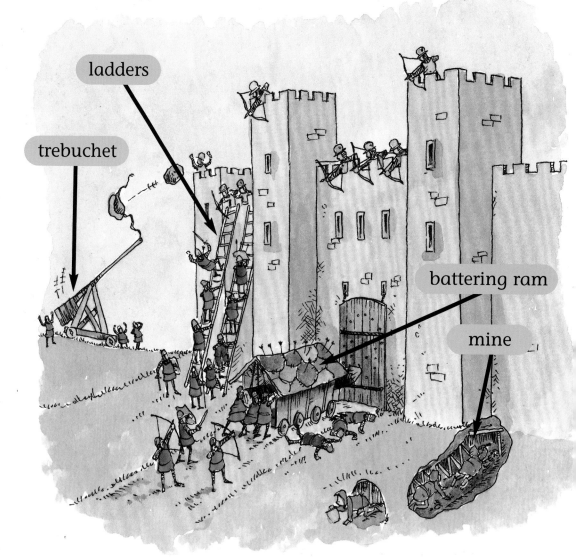

ladders

trebuchet

battering ram

mine

▲ *This castle is under attack.*

murder hole

portcullis

drawbridge

door

▲ *It wasn't easy to get into a castle!*

11

If the enemy couldn't break into the castle, they would besiege it. This meant the people inside couldn't go out, so they had to make sure they had enough food and drink inside the castle.

food

What did people need to survive a siege?

water

Food which didn't go off could be stored in the storeroom.

storeroom

kitchen

Wells were often very deep.

well

13

If enemies did break into the castle,
they had to be caught.

▲ *The stairs curled this way so that the soldier defending the castle could fight with the sword in his right hand.*

Enemies were locked up in dark, smelly dungeons.

castle dungeons

The garderobe

The castle lavatory was called the garderobe.
The window let fresh air in, but rain and
snow blew in too.

passage

garderobe

The passage kept
horrible smells
away from
the other rooms.

Castle windows

The shape of the windows shows
what they were used for.

Arrow slit

Hall window

Chapel window

Gun port

People began to use
guns and cannons from
about the year 1350.

At peace

In peaceful times, the castle's great hall was used for feasts. People slept there as well. Farmers came there to pay rents to their lord.

doorways to bedrooms

great hall – for feasts

fireplace

Castles today

A few castles are still used today.

▲ *Tower of London*

Some castles were destroyed by enemies.

▲ *Pontefract Castle*

Sometimes people took stones from the walls to build houses and now little is left.

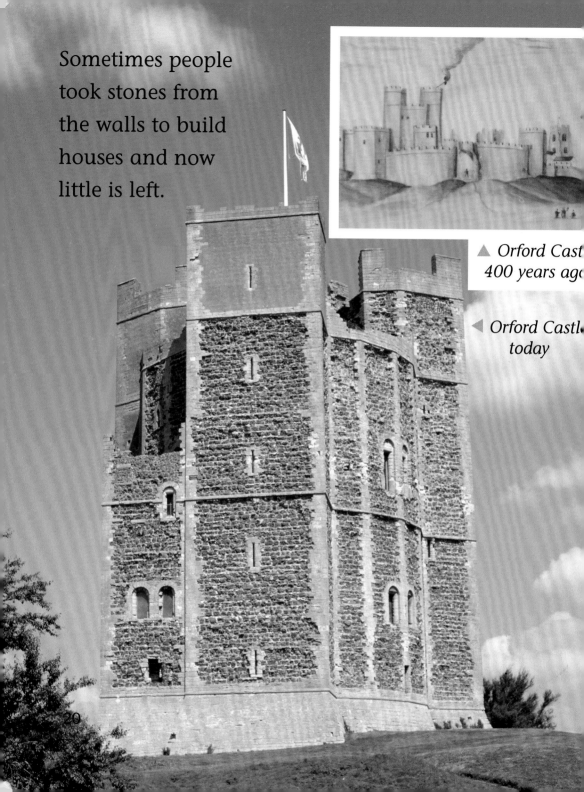

▲ Orford Castl[e] 400 years ago

◀ Orford Castl[e] today

20

Index

 crenel   8, 9

 mine   10

 drawbridge   11

 stairs   14

 fireplace   18

 tower   9

 garderobe   16

 windows   17

 hall   18

A castle

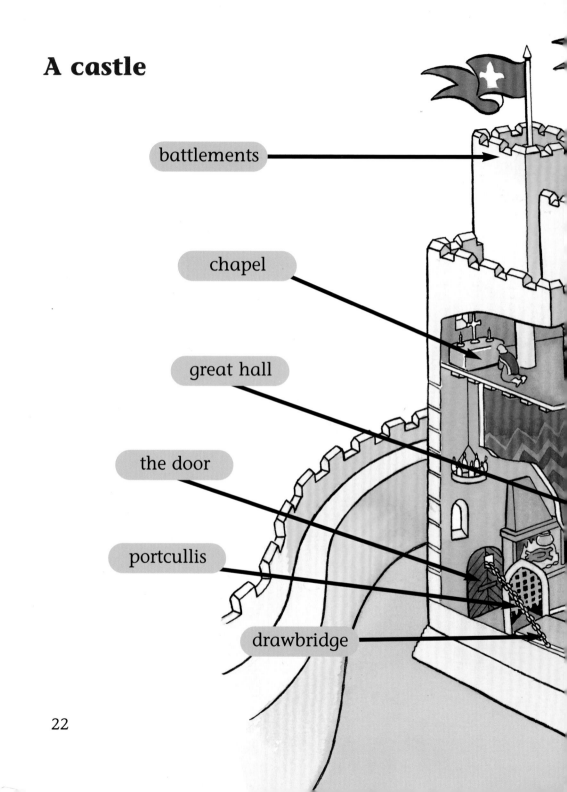

battlements

chapel

great hall

the door

portcullis

drawbridge

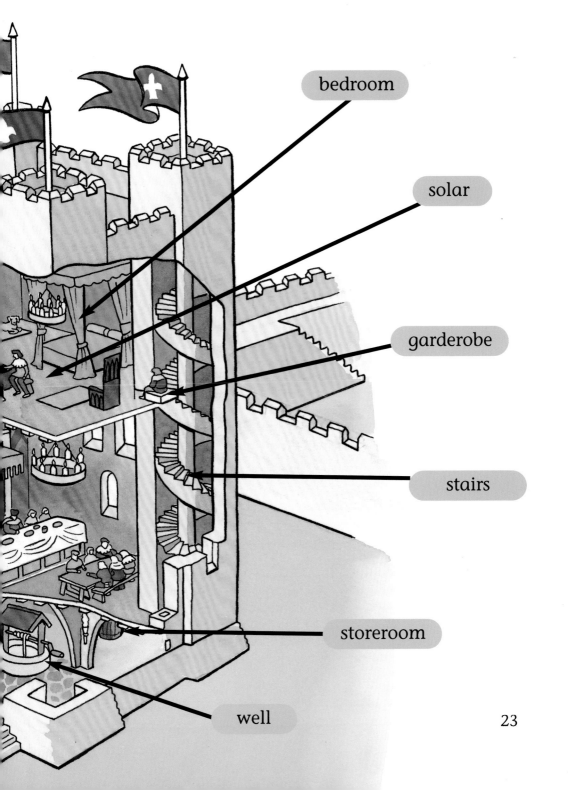

bedroom

solar

garderobe

stairs

storeroom

well

23

Ideas for reading

Written by Linda Pagett B.Ed(hons), M.Ed
Lecturer and Educational Consultant

Learning objectives: pose questions and record these in writing; use a contents page and index to find a way around text; scan text to find specific sections; use new words from reading linked to particular topics; present work from different parts of the curriculum for members of the class.

Curriculum links: Art and Design: Can buildings speak?; History: Famous events (Norman invasion)

High frequency words: did, where, were, so would, have, live, they, way, from, out, not, out, had, make, if

Interest words: moat, besiége, garderobe, drawbridge, portcullis, solar, battlements

Word count: 223

Resources: whiteboard and pens

Getting started

- Look at the cover together. Ask the children what they already know about castles and make a note of any unusual words they use such as *moat*. Ask them what they would like to find out about castles and write questions on the whiteboard.

- Using the contents page, discuss as a group where the answers to these questions might be and investigate. Ask the children to suggest headings to explore, and then turn and discuss what is on the pages.

- Using the index on page 21, give each child an area to research and then ask them to explain what they found out to the person sitting next to them.

Reading and responding

- Ask the children to read quietly and independently. They could use the contents and index pages to find the areas they wish to research. Listen in to each child reading in turn as the others continue working, praising good use of strategies for working out unfamiliar or tricky words.

- Ask each child to report back to the group on their findings, reading the relevant section, and outlining information they found out.

Castles

Maggie Freeman
Pat Murray   Mike Phillips

Collins Big Cat

Published by Collins
An imprint of HarperCollins*Publishers*
77–85 Fulham Palace Road
Hammersmith
London
W6 8JB

Browse the complete Collins catalogue at
www.collinseducation.com

Text © Maggie Freeman 2005
Illustrations and design © HarperCollins*Publishers* Limited 2005

Series editor: Cliff Moon

12

ISBN 978 0 00 718600 6

Maggie Freeman asserts her moral right to be identified as the author of this work.

British Library Cataloguing in Publication Data
A Catalogue record for this publication is available from the British Library.

Illustrators: Pat Murray, Mike Phillips
Design manager: Nikki O'Reilly, www.together-design.com
Guided reading ideas author: Linda Pagett

Acknowledgements
Photographs: Front cover: Alamy/Jon Arnold Images/Rex Butcher; p4, top: Corbis/Adam Woolfitt; p4, bottom: Courtesy of Manx National Heritage; p5, top: Alamy/Bill Wymar; p5, bottom: Corbis/Derek Croucher; p8, 9: Alamy/Jon Arnold Images/Rex Butcher; p11, bottom: Steve Crampton; p19, bottom: Steve Crampton; p19, top: Corbis/London Aerial Photo Library/Sandy Stockwell; p20: Corbis/Cordaiy Photo Library Ltd/John Howard; p20, inset: with kind permission of the New Orford Town Trust

Collins would like to thank the teachers and children at the following schools who took part in the development of Collins Big Cat:

Alfred Sutton Primary School
St. Anne's Fulshaw C of E Primary School
Anthony Bek Primary School
Biddick Primary School
Britannia Primary School
Christ Church Charnock Richard C of E Primary School
Cronton C of E Primary School
Cuddington Community School
Glory Farm County Primary and Nursery School

St. John Fisher RC Primary School
Killinghall Primary School
Malvern Link C of E Primary School
Margaret Macmillan Primary School
Minet Nursery and Infant School
Norbreck Primary School
Offley Endowed Primary School
Portsdown Primary School
St. Margaret's RC Primary School
Wadebridge Community Primary School

Printed in China by South China Printing Company Ltd.

Get the latest Collins Big Cat news at
www.collinsbigcat.com

Mixed Sources
Product group from well-managed forests and other controlled sources
www.fsc.org Cert no. SW-COC-1806
© 1996 Forest Stewardship Council
FSC